On Safari

Written and photographed by Jonathan and Angela Scott

Contents

Our home in Kenya

me and Angie

I'm Jonathan Scott, and I live with my wife Angie in Kenya. Our house is a short drive away from the middle of Nairobi, Kenya's capital city. But even though we live so close to the city, we are even closer to wild animals. Sometimes we meet a spotted **hyena** loping along the dirt road leading to our house, or pick out the giant shape of a giraffe walking past our front gate, and on a clear evening we can sometimes hear the mighty roar of lions.

herds of **wildebeest** feeding in the Nairobi National Park, Kenya

AFRICA

Kenya

Nairobi

Warthogs burrow under the fence to raid our vegetable garden.

Once a warthog attacked and injured one of our dogs with its sharp tusks.

warthogs feeding in our garden

The reason that we see wild animals so close to our home is that we live just a five-minute drive from Nairobi National Park, where lions and rhinos roam freely within sight of Nairobi's skyscrapers. And at the end of our road, within view of the beautiful Ngong Hills, is a private **game reserve** that is home to the endangered Rothschild's giraffe.

a leopard in search of food

three rare Rothschild's giraffes at the Giraffe Centre, Nairobi

There's always something exciting going on in our neighbourhood, like the time our neighbour had to rescue one of his dogs after it was **ambushed** by a leopard. Leopards often kill dogs and **jackals** for food.

4

Our house is built of stone and we have a huge garden. Some of it we've left wild and there's a dam where birds come to swim and drink in the rainy season. We have four dogs – Mara, Coco, Slippers and Artemis – and a cat called Little Cat. She was an orphan, found in our garage when she was very tiny. We really miss our animals when we're on safari, but our daughter, Alia, lives close by and she keeps an eye on things while we're away.

Angie and our dog, Artemis

our home in Langata, Nairobi

Little Cat in the garden

5

What is "on safari"?

We spend much of our time on safari. "Safari" is a beautiful Swahili word – Swahili is the language most commonly spoken in Kenya and East Africa. It means "journey", and when you say "safari", people think of a journey to Africa to see the wild animals, particularly the "big five": elephant, rhino, buffalo, lion and leopard.

tourists watching zebras

feeding time for baby orphan elephants at the Nairobi wildlife reserve

In the old days, a safari usually meant a journey to kill wild animals as trophies with guns, but hunting was banned in Kenya in 1977. Today, most people go on safari to enjoy seeing and photographing the wildlife, including animals under threat that have been rescued.

6

We go on safari all over the world, not just in Africa, but also in places like India and Antarctica so that we can photograph wildlife and share our experiences. We want people to see what amazing places there are in our world and to understand that everyone should protect our wild creatures.

penguins watching Angie as she gets ready to take a photo in Antarctica

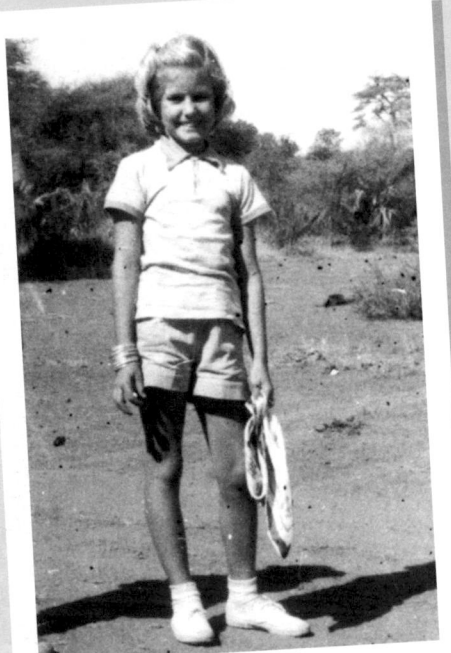

Angie as a girl in Tanzania

Angie has always loved photography. She was born in Africa and grew up in Tanzania, where there are many famous game parks. As a boy in England, I always dreamt of going on safari and when I grew up, I went in a truck going overland from London all the way to South Africa. That journey took nearly four months and by the time it ended I wanted to make Africa my home. I settled in Kenya and became a wildlife photographer, author and TV presenter. Big cats had always been my favourite animals, and my work gave me the chance to get to know them even better.

I always knew that if I truly wanted to understand wild animals, I would have to live where they live – in the wild. That is what Angie and I do when we go on safari.

me on my overland trip from London to South Africa

Travelling in the bush

Travelling to wild places like the Masai Mara game reserve often means
following dirt tracks and driving off-road for many hours, and we
sometimes have to make our own pathway with our vehicle.

driving off-road on the way to
the Masai Mara Game Park, Kenya

Our vehicle

To travel safely in the "bush" – that is the name people give the wilderness where wild animals live – we need a vehicle with four-wheel drive, often called a four-by-four (4 x 4). Four-wheel drive means that, if necessary, the engine can give power to all four wheels – most cars only power two wheels.

Four-wheel drive helps us to drive in mud and sand and through places that are wet and slippery after a rainstorm, where we would get stuck if we were driving an ordinary car. Even so, the tracks are so rough that sometimes we do get stuck.

Our four-by-four takes us everywhere, even when the road seems to disappear.

We often used to travel by ourselves in a four-by-four which was fitted out so that we could spend long periods in the bush. That way, we could make the best use of our chances of photographing animals. It's frustrating to have to go home, just as something wonderful is about to happen.

When I was photographing wild dogs and the wildebeest migration, I'd carry enough supplies to live for weeks at a time in my car. Sometimes I wouldn't see another person for many days. This way, I could follow the animals as they moved about, without returning to a fixed camp each day.

wildebeest crossing the Mara river, Kenya

me camping in the bush

We once had a car that we had specially made for us. It had been a **pick-up**, but we covered over the back so we could sleep in it. We made special doors so that we could use our equipment easily and have more room to work. The doors had **mounts** fitted on them, so we could move our cameras in any direction. This way, we could best capture the action when the animals started moving around.

The cameras are mounted on the open windows of our doors, to keep them steady as we follow an animal.

Photographing out of the roof hatches allows us to see exactly what's around us.

It's important for us to have a car with roof hatches. These are holes cut in the roof of the car – one over the driver's seat and two further back. They allow us to stand up through the roof of the car and photograph all around. The animals in the game reserves very rarely attack tourists in cars, but it wouldn't be sensible to get out of the car and walk about if there were lions close by.

We're always ready to take a photo!

This young elephant wanted to play.

This ring-tailed lemur from Madagascar was *too* friendly.

Taking photos: our cameras

We're often away for weeks or months on safari, so it's important to carry enough cameras and lenses. That way, if one of them lets us down or breaks we have a back-up. Sometimes things get so frantic that I even drop cameras and lenses out of the vehicle!

We normally travel with up to six cameras and many different lenses so that we can shoot all kinds of different pictures – close-ups and distance shots, photos of animals running at top speed or lying still, in bright sunshine or deep shadow.

The African plains look green after the rain. Here we used a special lens to include as many animals as possible.

To take care of so much valuable and **fragile** camera equipment, we've sewn special **pouches** into the seat covers of our vehicle, each the right size for a different camera and lens. Once or twice we've come close to tipping the car over when we've hit a warthog burrow or **termite mound**, and the pouches help to stop our equipment getting dusty or falling on the floor.

We use special rucksacks when we're photographing away from the vehicle. These make it easy to carry cameras and lenses on our backs. Everything can be packed carefully into its own compartment, protected with soft foam liners.

Here are our backpacks for carrying our equipment.

You can take great photos with a very simple camera, but for this close-up shot I needed a special lens. I couldn't safely go so near to a lion.

15

Using very long **telephoto** lenses, which act like binoculars, means that we don't get too close to the animals we want to photograph. This way we don't disturb them by making them upset or frightened. We can then record their normal behaviour when they're hunting, feeding and looking after their young.

I used a telephoto lens to take this picture. The lions didn't know they were on camera.

Here Angie used a special lens to get all these elephants into the picture.

It's important to keep the camera nice and steady, otherwise the photographs will be blurred. To prevent this, we use camera mounts and **tripods**. We also rest our cameras on canvas bags filled with beans or sand so they don't wobble about.

Life is easier now that our cameras are digital and we no longer use film. Films are bulky to carry. They can also get damaged by the heat, so we often had to keep them in a little fridge with our food.

17

What we take on safari

Water and food

When we're in the bush, we may end up very far away from any other people, camps or lodges, so it's important that we carry enough food and water. Water is especially important. You need plenty of water to drink because it's hot and it's dangerous if you get **dehydrated**. We always carry packets of salt and sugar powder to mix with water and make a special drink in case we get ill in the heat. This drink **rehydrates** our bodies.

We also need water for the radiator of the vehicle, so that the engine doesn't overheat. We fill large plastic containers with water and carry them on the front of the car as well as inside it.

We also take a supply of food and medicines.

breakfast cereals

vacuum flasks

cool box

pans

gas cooker

baked beans

long-life juice

mugs

toilet paper

pasta

salt

pepper

coffee

long-life milk

18

Fresh supplies come by air

There are no shops in the bush, so our daughter has to buy fresh supplies or new equipment in Nairobi and send them down to us by air. The same little plane also brings visitors and letters to wherever we're based.

a male lion relaxing on the runway

Computers

We each have a computer to make notes on what's been happening, and write our books and articles when we're in the bush. We also need the computer so that Angie can download our digital images.

We can charge the computer's battery with a device that plugs into the vehicle's cigarette lighter.

Angie working at her laptop

When you're waiting for something to happen, a warm drink makes a real difference.

Home comforts

We take a little gas cooker to prepare a hot meal and to brew a nice warming cup of tea or coffee in the morning, in the middle of the day and in the evening. We have lots of books to read, because we spend many hours waiting for animals to appear.

Leopards are especially shy, so we have to be particularly patient with them. Very early one morning some years ago, I spotted a leopard slinking into a cave. I waited over 12 hours before she came out for a few brief moments and I took photos that are still some of my favourites. Then she saw the car and froze, before slipping away into the darkness.

Leopards are very shy. This leopard stopped to stare at me before slipping away into the bushes.

Emergency supplies

We're sometimes a long way from any help, so we need to take medical supplies, and spares for the vehicle in case it breaks down. We carry extra tyres and inner tubes, and high-lift jacks to raise the car up when it gets stuck in a hole or in mud, or has a puncture. We also have a **winch** with a long steel cable fixed to the front of the vehicle, so we can attach it to a tree and pull ourselves out of trouble.

It's vital to keep two spare wheels in the car in case we get a puncture. Here, I'm trying to lift the car up with a jack.

Camping gear

When Angie and I work, we never know exactly where the animals we're photographing – cheetahs, leopards, wild dogs, lions, wildebeest – will lead us. We usually stay in a tented camp, which is like a permanent camping site, but sometimes we sleep in our four-by-four. This gives us the best chance of finding the animals we're working with again each morning, as we'll have slept close to where we left them the previous night. Even though it's often very hot in Africa during the daytime, it can be cold at night, so we need warm blankets, duvets, sleeping bags and extra clothes.

We often stay in tents like this one, at Film Camp in the Mara. Tented camps are very comfortable and we can have a wash or a shower. There are mosquito nets to keep away insects while we sleep.

Here we are staying at a tented camp. These tents are permanent. The canopy keeps off both the sun and the rain.

23

Danger in the wild

In game parks and reserves, animals are protected and we aren't allowed to carry guns to defend ourselves. The animals have right of way and it's up to us to make sure that we don't put ourselves in danger. Wild creatures usually want to be left in peace. They rarely attack unless scared or hungry or wounded.

Even so, Angie and I have had some scary moments. People often think that the big cats are the most dangerous animals we meet, and sometimes they can be, but buffaloes can be truly terrifying. Bull buffaloes can weigh up to a ton and are very quick and very powerful. They can kill lions and unlike most creatures, who attack and run away, angry buffaloes will fight to the death.

This lioness is scared of the buffalo.

These two angry buffaloes
are about to charge.

Hippos can also be very dangerous. It's said that hippos kill more people than lions. Never get between hippos and water, as they feel trapped if they can't run back to the safety of a lake or river.

One morning on the riverbank I bumped into a bull hippo. It charged and I ran back to my vehicle clicking off a photo over my shoulder, thinking, "At least everyone will know what happened if it tramples me!" I dodged round the back of my car.
The hippo hurtled round the front, grunting and gnashing its teeth and throwing up a huge cloud of dust. Luckily, it then lumbered off into the bushes.

A charging hippo can run faster than a man.

two male hippos fighting

Safari diary

Dawn

We often stay at a camp in the Masai Mara game reserve, called Governor's Camp. Here we can be close to the animals we photograph and follow them for days on end, recording their lives.

We like to leave camp early in the morning, so we can find the animals we want to photograph before the sun comes up. The light in the early morning and in the evening is very beautiful, and the colours look deeper and richer at these times.

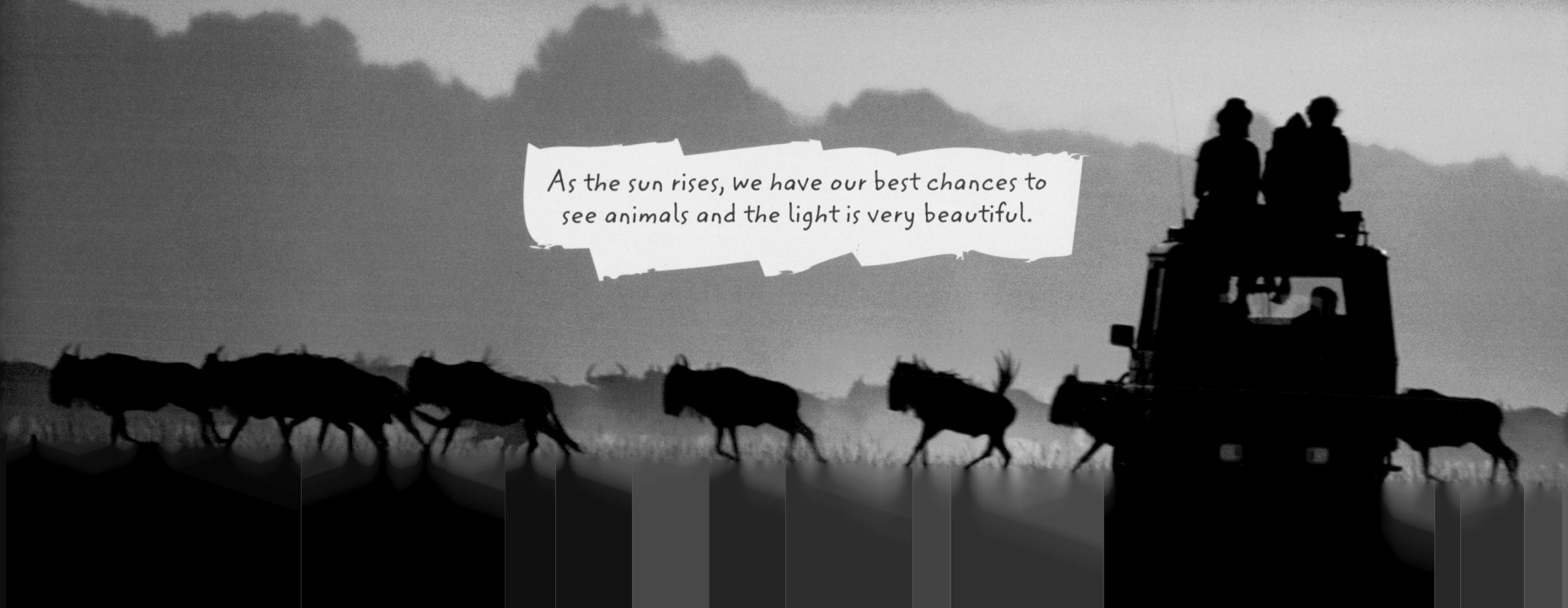

As the sun rises, we have our best chances to see animals and the light is very beautiful.

Animals such as the big cats prefer the cooler mornings and evenings. They're more active and easier to find at those times than in the heat of the day, when they're resting. Some of these big cats we've known for several years. We've watched their cubs and we've seen some of these cubs grow up to have cubs of their own.

a mother cheetah and her playful cubs at dawn

This male lion is waiting in the dawn light.

Midday

Nearly everyone rests in the heat of the day. It's too hot to do anything else.

However, we continue to keep a track of the animals we're photographing. One way to find them is to pick a high point early in the day – maybe the top of a ridge – and use binoculars to look around. Then it's usually best to stay still and wait, rather than rush about from place to place.

A high place is ideal for spotting animals.

Nearly everyone snoozes in the midday heat, including these leopards.

You have to use all your senses when you're looking for wild animals – you must look, listen and smell. Quite often, you'll hear lions roaring, or hyenas whooping and cackling. A swirl of **vultures** spiralling in the sky can signal the place where a **predator** has made a kill. If you hear monkeys or jackals calling in alarm, it often means they have spotted a leopard on the move. And if zebras are all standing alert and snorting they point you in the direction of where they've seen a predator – perhaps a cheetah.

Giraffe are one of the few animals that move about in the heat of the day.

Evening

Night comes very suddenly in Africa. Soon the darkness is alive with animals slinking warily down to a river or waterhole to drink. Gazelles and other prey animals usually drink earlier in the day unless they're in the safety of a herd. They're afraid to risk meeting the big cats at the start of a night's hunting.

zebras in the early evening light

Photographing cheetahs

Cheetahs are among our favourite animals. They hunt mainly during the daytime – unlike lions and leopards, which usually hunt when it's dark. By hunting during the day, cheetahs can avoid most of the larger and more dangerous predators, but they must always keep a wary eye out for spotted hyenas. Cheetahs are very beautiful and they're fantastic runners, but they aren't as physically strong as the hyenas or the other big cats. This is why cheetahs don't **scavenge** from the kills made by other predators. In fact, they sometimes lose their own kills to more powerful competitors.

Female cheetahs hunt alone and are especially at risk, because they have to protect their cubs and can't run away.

A hyena can kill cheetah cubs.

a mother cheetah taking her kill to her cubs

Fact box		
	Cheetahs	Lions
Adult weight	31-64 kilogrammes	120-220 kilogrammes
Life span	8-12 years	12-15+ years
Top speed	100-120 kilometres per hour	60 kilometres per hour

The cheetah is the fastest land animal on Earth.

We've followed the lives of several cheetahs and one of our favourites was a mother cheetah called Honey. We got to know her well as we watched her cubs grow up. Honey used to spend most of her time close to the grassy slopes of Rhino Ridge, in the Masai Mara game reserve.

She liked it there because she could find plenty of food, particularly Thomson's gazelles which live out on the plains and feed on the sweet green grasses. Gazelles are fast, but cheetahs are the swiftest land animals on Earth. We're always trying to capture, on camera, the moments when a cheetah sprints after a gazelle in a high-speed chase.

Young gazelles are the easiest prey as they aren't as quick and strong as the adults. They spend much of the time lying with chin to the ground, hiding from predators such as Honey.

a baby gazelle with its mother

Cheetahs rely on their speed to catch their prey.
This baby gazelle is trying to dodge out of danger.

We loved the times when Honey had cubs, as she was always busy, keeping them safe from danger, providing food and teaching them the skills they needed to become successful hunters. Cheetah mothers are very caring, licking and grooming their cubs just like our house cat does with her kittens. Honey was a very good mother, but it's incredibly difficult for a mother cheetah to raise her cubs.

Life is dangerous for young cheetahs because there are many predators and few safe places to hide on the open plains. Many cheetahs don't manage to raise more than one or two cubs in a lifetime.

A mother cheetah and her cubs are using this tree as a high point to watch the plains. Here, they are also safe from predators like hyenas who can't climb.

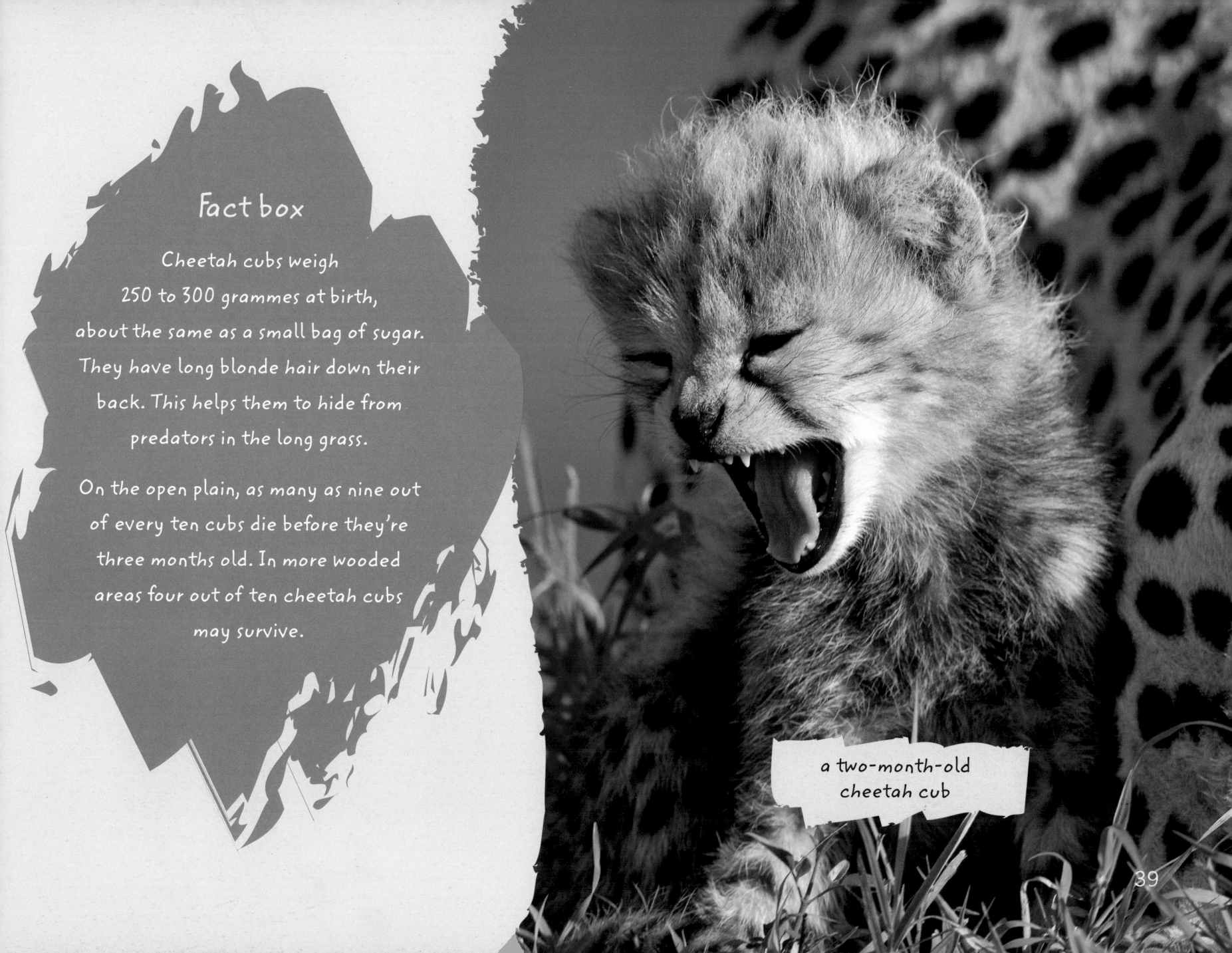

Fact box

Cheetah cubs weigh
250 to 300 grammes at birth,
about the same as a small bag of sugar.
They have long blonde hair down their
back. This helps them to hide from
predators in the long grass.

On the open plain, as many as nine out
of every ten cubs die before they're
three months old. In more wooded
areas four out of ten cheetah cubs
may survive.

a two-month-old
cheetah cub

Cheetahs like Honey are completely relaxed with vehicles, because they grew up with tourists driving around their home. Sometimes a cheetah drags her kill under our car or seeks shade for herself and her cubs in the heat of the day. When she does this you can hear her panting or purring to her cubs – cheetahs can purr very loudly.

A mother cheetah has dragged her kill to our car for safety. She waits and watches while her cubs are feeding.

This cheetah is not afraid of our car.

40

Soon the cubs are confident with vehicles, too. Young cheetah cubs will play under a safari vehicle, and as they become bigger and stronger they may even try to climb on to it. They love the tyres because they have a rough surface to grip on. Often, they'll scramble on to the roof and sit there contentedly, gazing out across the plains. If they're really relaxed, they'll lie down and have a nap. This may seem strange – but cheetahs also like climbing on to termite mounds or fallen trees. They need a good view of their surroundings so they can spot danger or the chance to hunt. They can also leave scent messages for other cheetahs to find.

We've spent up to 14 hours a day with the cheetahs, and, watching their triumphs and misfortunes, we feel that we've come to know them. Many evenings it's hard to stop photographing, and we're always excited to see what the following morning will bring. It's also hard not to worry about them. Life is tough for these remarkable cats and we're full of admiration for creatures like them.

But at last it's time to leave the Masai Mara.
We must pack up and set off back to Nairobi with
our photos and the notes for our new books.
We're looking forward to getting home, but we're
also sad to say goodbye to the game reserve and
all the creatures whose lives we've shared.

Glossary

ambushed   suddenly and unexpectedly attacked

dehydrated   dangerously short of water

fragile   easily damaged

game reserve   an area of land set aside for animals to live in undisturbed

hyena   an animal that looks a bit like a dog and hunts in a pack

jackals   fox-like animals that will sometimes follow big cats in the hope of stealing their prey, but risk being killed by them

mounts   pieces of equipment that can be used to attach cameras to a vehicle

pick-up   a vehicle with a cab for the driver and passengers, and an open back with low sides for carrying things

pouches   pockets usually made out of fabric, for storing things in

predator   a meat-eating animal that hunts other creatures for food

rehydrates   gets more water back into your body

scavenge   take food from other animals

telephoto   a special lens that makes distant objects look much closer than they are

termite mound   a mound-shaped nest, often 2 or 3 metres high, with solid walls that small insects called termites make from soil, mud and chewed-up wood

tripods   three-legged stands used to hold cameras steady

vultures   large birds with curved beaks, that live off the remains of dead animals

warthogs   fierce wild African pigs with curved tusks

wildebeest   grass-eating animals, distantly related to cows and goats, that live in herds and have to travel great distances every year to find new pastures

winch   a piece of equipment that winds a rope or a cable around a drum, in order to pull heavy objects along

Index

A day on safari

5:00 to 5:30 a.m.

We wake to the sound of lions and the honking grunts of hippos from the river nearby. Time to pull on our clothes and grab a quick cup of tea (coffee for Angie to kick-start her day) and a biscuit. This may be our last food until around 2:00 p.m. We unzip the tent and the sky is clear, stars still twinkling.

setting off at dawn

6:00 a.m.

We load all the cameras into their bags and start up the vehicle. We always feel excited at this point. What will we see today?

6:15 a.m.

Today we meet lions right outside camp. One of the female lions has made a kill and the cubs are joining in the feast. The sun is coming up and that first ten minutes of golden orange light is exquisite. Photographing is difficult as there is not much light yet and light is vital for sharp, clear photos. Soon other animals gather to share the food and vultures will take what's left.

lions with a kill

8:30 a.m.

The lions, leopards and hyenas settle down for the day somewhere shady. We're in luck! We find a mother cheetah and her cubs and watch while she goes hunting. But she misses a young gazelle. The cubs will have to wait a little longer for their food.

12:00 noon to 3:00 p.m.
Blinding heat in the middle of the day and we drink lots of water. Spending 14 hours in a vehicle can be tough. We've always got to be alert to make sure we don't miss anything.

5:30 p.m.
Suddenly the mother cheetah dashes after a gazelle and after a high-speed chase she catches it. She calls to her cubs to let them know that it's safe to leave their hiding place. Now they won't go hungry — but our cheetah family have to eat quickly before it gets dark and other predators start hunting.

The waterhole is where we can expect to find animals, like these elephants.

a cheetah chasing a gazelle

6:00 p.m.
At the waterhole, the elephants come down to drink. We especially love to see baby elephants playing in the water. Sometimes they even get told off by their mothers! We don't want to leave, but night falls swiftly in the African bush. It's time to get back. Tired, but with our heads buzzing with all the amazing things we've seen, we go back to camp to wash off the dust of another long day in the bush.

47

 Ideas for reading

Written by Clare Dowdall BA(Ed), MA(Ed)
Lecturer and Primary Literacy Consultant

Learning objectives: use knowledge of different organisational features of texts to find information effectively; explain how writers use figurative and expressive language to create images and atmosphere; take different roles in groups and use the language appropriate to them, including the roles of leader, reporter, scribe and mentor; develop scripts based on improvisation

Curriculum links: Geography: Passport to the world; Art and Design: Journeys; Citizenship: Animals and us

Interest words: ambushed, dehydrated, fragile, game reserve, predator, rehydrates, scavenge, telephoto, tripods, wide-angle, winch

Resources: ICT, whiteboards, notebooks

Getting started

This book can be read over two or more guided reading sessions.

- Look at the front and back covers. Discuss what the word *safari* might mean.

- Read the blurb to the children. Find Kenya in an atlas or on a globe and discuss what it might be like there.

- As a group, discuss the blurb questions: *What's it really like to go on a safari? What do you take? What will you find?*

- In pairs, ask children to make a list of what they would take with them to Kenya for a safari.

- Identify how the blurb is written to attract the reader's interest.

Reading and responding

- In pairs, read chapter 1 (pp2–5). Ask children to note any new words and any words that the authors use to interest the reader and create atmosphere.

- Model how to use the glossary to deepen understanding of words like *hyena* and *warthogs*.

- Ask children to use the contents page to choose a chapter to read independently. Support children to locate information, and make meaning as they read.

Returning to the book

- Ask each child to tell a partner about the chapter that they read. In pairs, ask children to find the words that the authors have used to make the chapters interesting and record them.

- Model how to present information from reading, using powerful language and making reference to the text.